W9-AVN-535

Reading Maps

**Marta Segal Block and
Daniel R. Block**

Heinemann Library
Chicago, IL

©2008 **Heinemann Library**
a division of Reed Elsevier Inc.
Chicago, Illinois

Customer Service 888-454-2279
Visit our website at **www.heinemannlibrary.com**

Designed by Jennifer Lacki, Kimberly R. Miracle, and Betsy Wernert

Illustrations by Mapping Specialists

Originated by Modern Age

Printed and bound in China by South China Printing Co. Ltd.

12 11 10 09 08
10 9 8 7 6 5 4 3 2 1
10-digit ISBNs: 1-4329-0792-1 (hc); 1-4329-0798-0 (pb)

Library of Congress Cataloging-in-Publication Data

Block, Marta Segal.
  Reading maps / Marta Segal Block and Daniel R. Block.
     p. cm. -- (First guide to maps)
  Includes bibliographical references and index.
  ISBN-13: 978-1-4329-0792-1 (hc : alk. paper)
  ISBN-13: 978-1-4329-0798-3 (pb : alk. paper) 1. Map reading--Juvenile literature. I. Block,
     Daniel, 1967- II. Title.
  GA130.B56 2008
  912.01′4--dc22
                           2007048621

Acknowledgments
The author and publishers are grateful to the following for permission to reproduce copyright
material: ©Corbis pp. **10** (zefa/ Jason Horowitz); **13b** (Royalty Free); ©drr.net/Stock Connection
p. **9** (Mark & Audrey Gibson); ©Getty Images pp. **12a** (Royalty Free), **13a** (Royalty Free);
©istockphoto pp. **12b** (Björn Kindler), **27** (roberta casaliggi); ©Map Resources p. **4**; ©NASA p. **26**.

Cover design by Kimberly R. Miracle and Jennifer Lacki

Every effort has been made to contact copyright holders of any material reproduced
in this book. Any omissions will be rectified in subsequent printings if notice is given
to the publisher.

Contents

Any words appearing in the text in bold, **like this**, are explained in the glossary.

What Are Maps?

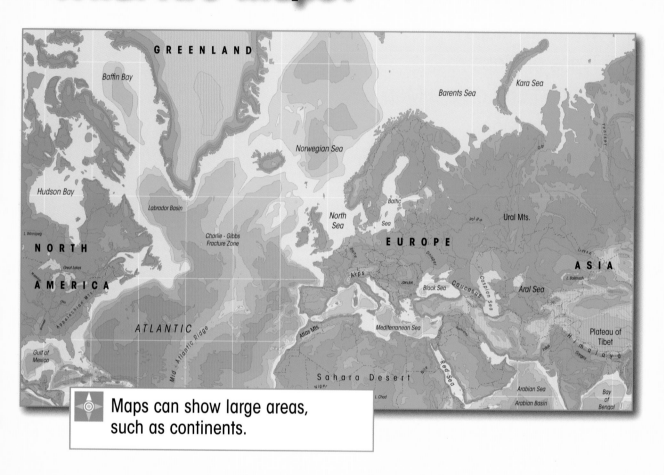

Maps can show large areas, such as continents.

A map is a flat drawing of a part of the world. People who make maps are called **cartographers**.

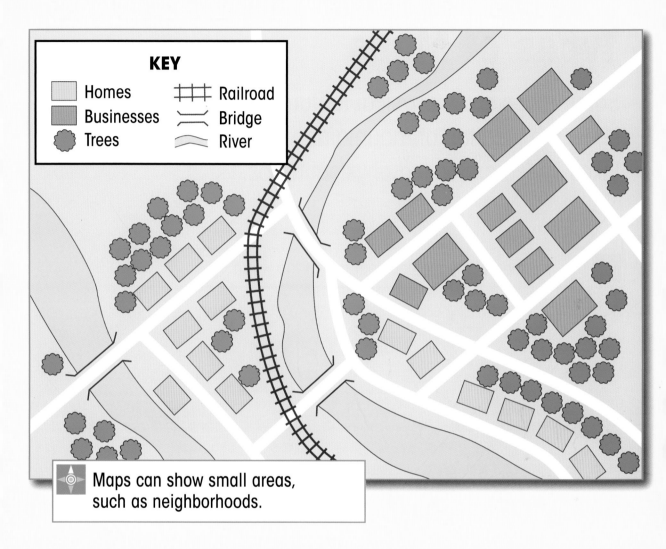

KEY

▢	Homes	⫢	Railroad
▢	Businesses	⟩⟨	Bridge
✿	Trees	～	River

Maps can show small areas, such as neighborhoods.

We use maps to find the location of places. We use them to study physical features such as mountains or lakes. We also use them to learn more about people.

Types of Maps

Some maps show physical features of the land. They show the location of mountains, valleys, rivers, and lakes. These are called physical maps.

This is a map of the physical features of the world.

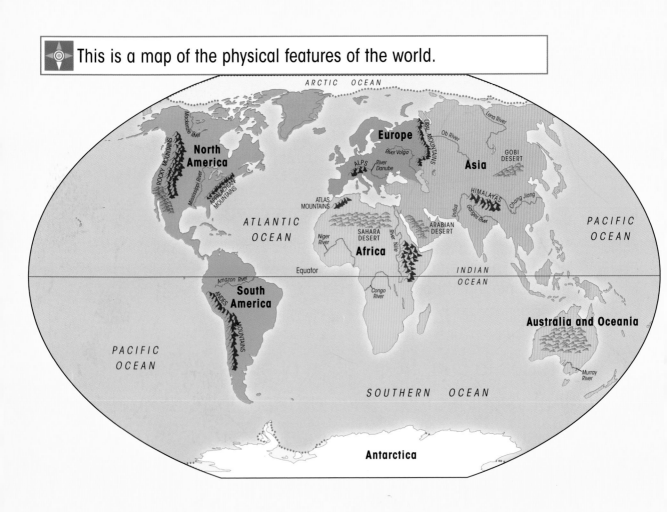

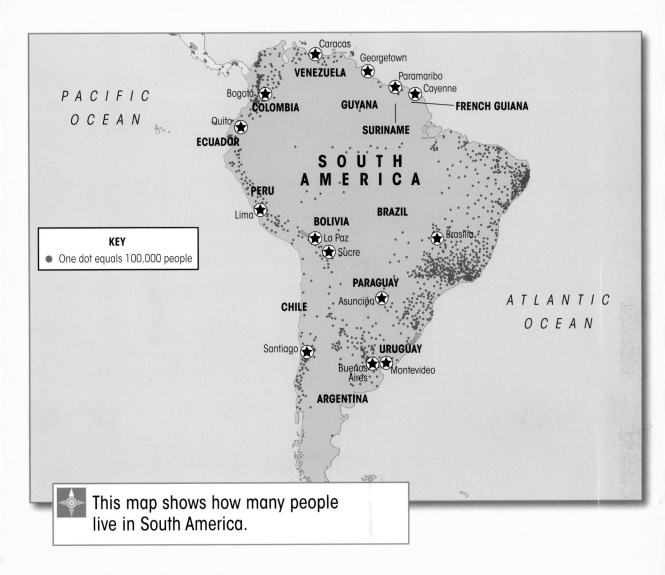

KEY

● One dot equals 100,000 people

Caracas
Georgetown
VENEZUELA
Paramaribo
Bogotá
Cayenne
COLOMBIA
GUYANA
FRENCH GUIANA
Quito
SURINAME
ECUADOR

SOUTH
AMERICA

PERU
Lima
BRAZIL
BOLIVIA
La Paz
Brasília
Sucre

PARAGUAY
CHILE
Asunción

ATLANTIC
OCEAN

PACIFIC
OCEAN

Santiago
URUGUAY
Buenos
Montevideo
Aires

ARGENTINA

This map shows how many people
live in South America.

Some maps show information about people and where
they live. They show the location of cities, roads, and
airports. They show the **borders** between countries. They
can also show how many people live in an area.

Fitting Earth onto a Map

You may wonder how mapmakers fit the round Earth on a flat map. Try this activity: Use a marker to draw some lines and circles on the skin of an orange. Now peel the orange and try to make the skin of the orange lay flat. Notice how the size and shape of your drawings have changed. You have to push and pull the peel to flatten it.

To fit Earth's features onto a map, **cartographers** "push" and "pull" in a similar way. They change the shape and size of things on Earth. Then they can fit them onto a map.

Cartographers choose which features of Earth they must change to fit them onto a map.

Reading Maps

Maps have many features to help you read them.

Map title

Most maps have a title. The title tells what the map is about. The title could be the name of a location. It could also tell about the type of information shown.

Compass Rose

Many maps have a **compass rose**. This feature shows the **cardinal directions**. The cardinal directions are north, south, east, and west.

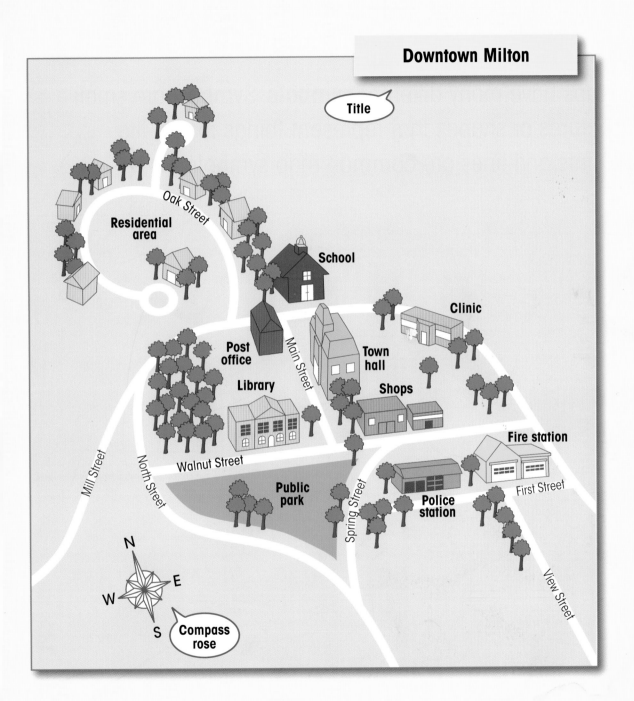

Downtown Milton

Title

Residential area

Oak Street

School

Clinic

Post office

Town hall

Main Street

Library

Shops

Fire station

Mill Street

North Street

Walnut Street

Public park

Spring Street

Police station

First Street

View Street

N
W E
S

Compass rose

Map Symbols

Maps have many different **symbols**. Symbols are small pictures or shapes that represent things in real life. Points and lines are common map symbols.

Dots often represent cities. Lines on a map may represent roads.

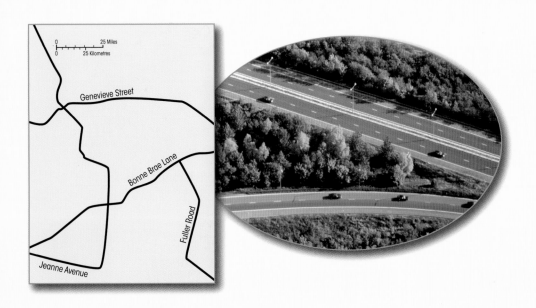

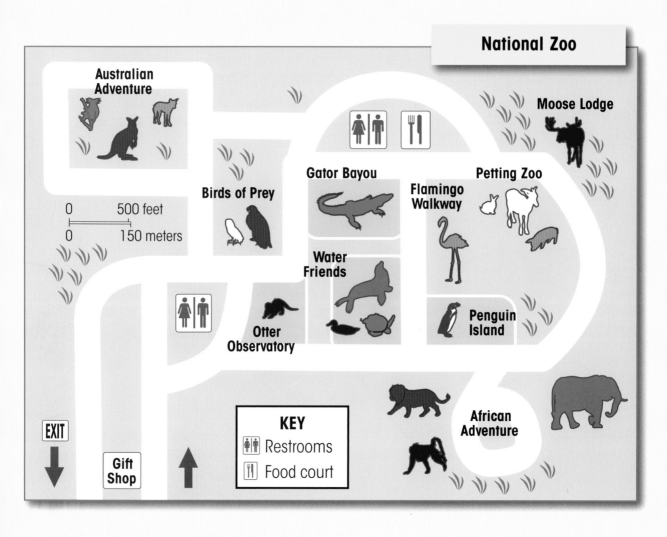

Some **symbols** on a map look like the things they represent. On the map above, pictures of animals show their location in a zoo.

Map key

Symbols can be different from map to map. That is why maps have a **key**. This feature tells what the symbols on the map mean.

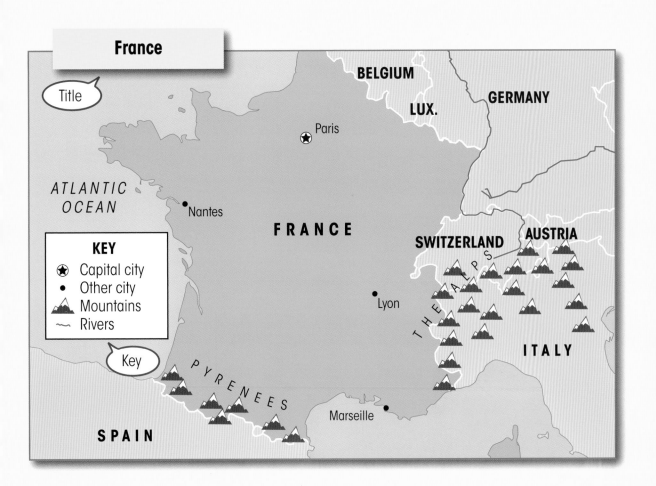

Using color

Some maps use color to show different areas. States and countries are often shown with different colors. The map below uses color to show different buildings.

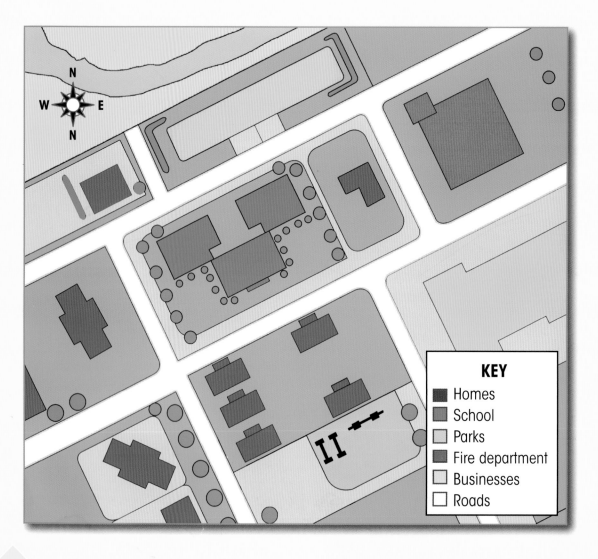

KEY
- Homes
- School
- Parks
- Fire department
- Businesses
- Roads

Scale

Most maps have a **scale**. This feature can be used to measure distance. The scale shows how many miles or kilometers are represented by every inch or centimeter.

You can use the scale to measure distance.

Large and Small

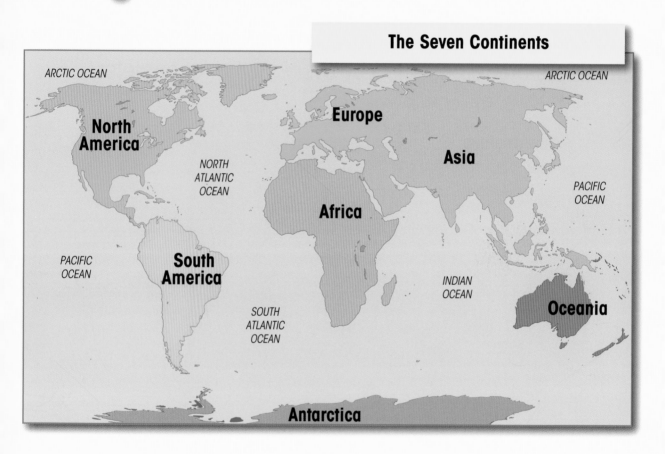

The Seven Continents

ARCTIC OCEAN

North America

NORTH ATLANTIC OCEAN

Europe

Asia

ARCTIC OCEAN

PACIFIC OCEAN

Africa

PACIFIC OCEAN

South America

SOUTH ATLANTIC OCEAN

INDIAN OCEAN

Oceania

Antarctica

Some maps show a very large area, such as a **continent**. These maps may only show **borders** between countries and large bodies of water.

Some maps show a smaller area, such as a city or town. These maps include many details. They show the location of parks, streets, museums, and hospitals.

This map shows downtown Atlanta, Georgia.

KEY
- Building
- ◆ Place of Interest

Western Av.
Jones Av.
Simpson St.

TECHWOOD

Mills St.
Alexander St.
W. Peachtree Pl.
Simpson St.

Luckie St.
Venable St.
McAfee St.
Lovejoy St.

◆ Aquarium

Park Av. West

OLYMPIC

PARK

Centennial Olympic Park Dr.
Williams St.
Spring St.
Peachtree St.

Baker St.

Harris St.

Convention Center

Andrew Young International Blvd.

FAIRLIE
POPLAR

Peachtree Center Av.
Courtland St.
Piedmont Av.

Ellis St.

CNN
Center

Luckie St.
Poplar St.
Wallon St.
Marietta St.

J.W. Dobbs Av.

Museum

Philips
Arena

PLAZA

Techwood

WOODRUFF

PARK

Auburn Av.

CASTLEBERRY
HILL

Edgewood Av.

Martin Luther King Jr. Dr.

Decatur St.
Wall St.
Alabama St.

HURT
PARK

Courtland St.

Spring St.
Forsyth St.
Broad St.
Peachtree St.
Martin Luther King Jr. Dr.
Pryor St.
Central Av.

Piedmont Av.
Gilmer St.
Jesse Hill Jr. Dr.

Mitchell St.

Map scale

0   1/8   1/4 Mile
0   1/8   1/4 Kilometer

Trinity Av.

◆ State Capitol

GRANT
PARK

Lines Around the World

Some maps have lines on them that divide the world into parts. Two important lines are the **Equator** and the **Prime Meridian**.

The Equator is an imaginary line that runs across Earth. It is halfway between the North Pole and the South Pole.

The Prime Meridian is an imaginary line that runs from the top to the bottom of Earth. It goes from the North Pole to the South Pole. Together, these imaginary lines divide the world into four parts.

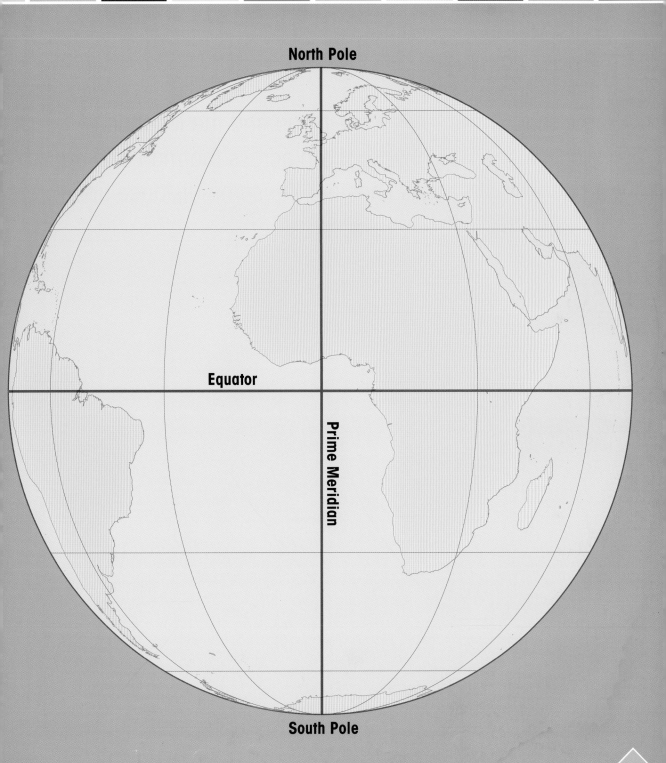

North Pole

Equator

Prime Meridian

South Pole

Map Grids

Some maps use a **grid** to help you find the location of a place. A grid has lines that run across the map and up and down the map. All lines are the same distance apart.

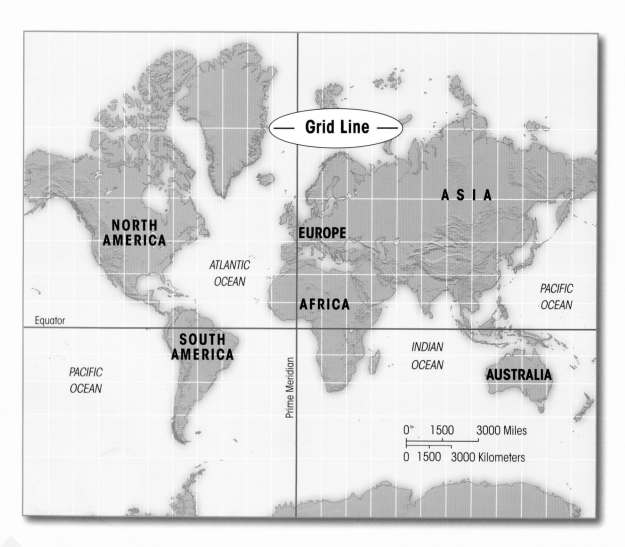

Grid Line

ASIA

NORTH
AMERICA

EUROPE

ATLANTIC
OCEAN

PACIFIC
OCEAN

AFRICA

Equator

SOUTH
AMERICA

INDIAN
OCEAN

Prime Meridian

AUSTRALIA

PACIFIC
OCEAN

0   1500   3000 Miles

0   1500   3000 Kilometers

City maps often have a grid. This type of grid has letters along one side of the map and numbers along the other. The lines from a letter and a number come together to show the exact location of a place.

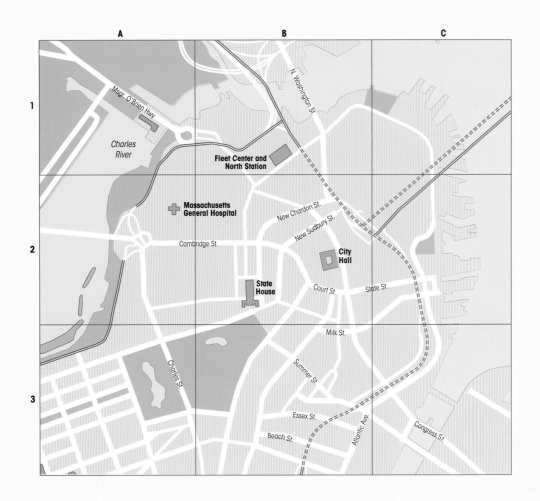

Latitude and Longitude

A special type of **grid** shows the exact location of places. This grid is called **latitude** and **longitude**.

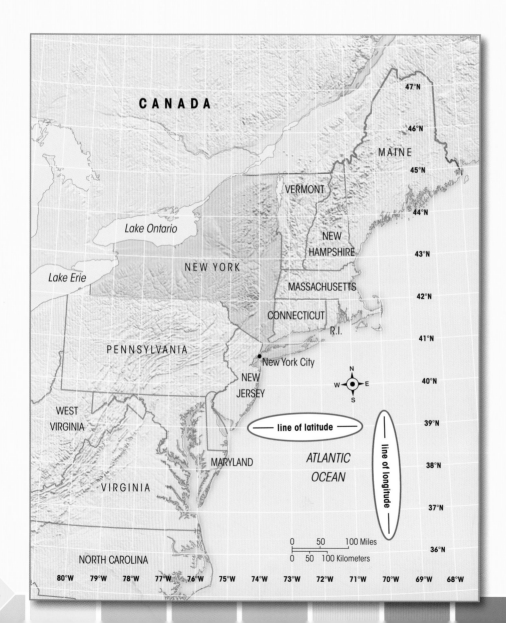

Latitude tells you how far north or south you are from the **Equator**. Latitude lines run across the map. Longitude tells you how far east or west you are from the **Prime Meridian**. Longitude lines run up and down the map.

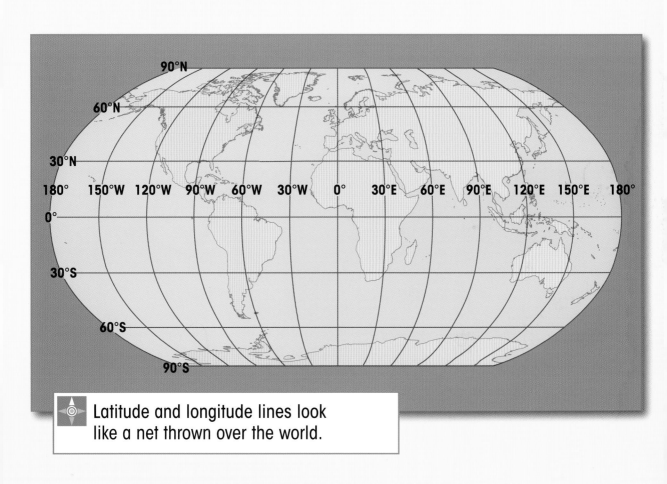

Latitude and longitude lines look like a net thrown over the world.

Making Maps

In the past, **cartographers** used special tools to draw maps. Today, they can use computers to help them draw maps. They can also use images from **satellites**. Satellites take pictures of Earth from space.

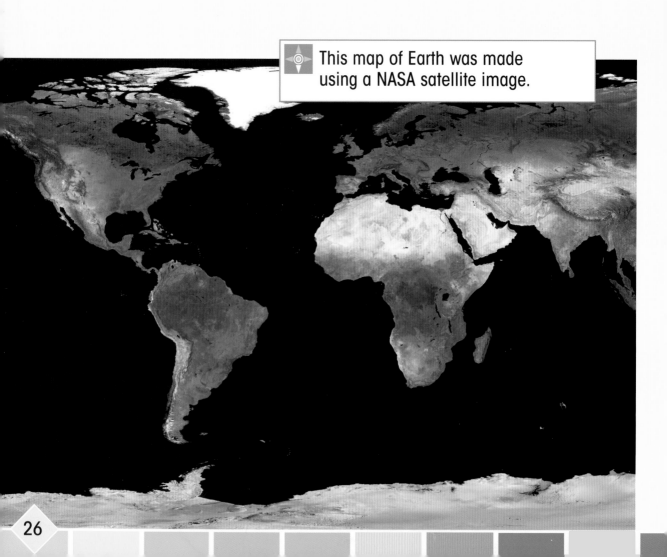

This map of Earth was made using a NASA satellite image.

Some cars have a GPS that shows driving directions.

Cartographers also use the **Global Positioning System (GPS)**. GPS is a computer network that collects pictures from satellites high above Earth. GPS can tell people exactly where they are and how to get from one place to another. Mapmakers can also use GPS to draw the exact location of places on a map.

Maps are an important part of our lives. They can show us all kinds of information about the world we live in.

Map Activities

Activity 1: Map Collection

1. Collect as many different maps as you can. Examples of maps you might be able to collect are bus routes, zoo maps, and city maps.

2. Think about local businesses that may have maps. For example, the bank may have a map that shows where ATMs are located. Your doctor may have a map showing the way to the hospital.

3. Look at the maps and discuss or write the ways the maps are different and alike. Why do the maps look different?

Activity 2: Create a Map

Draw a map of an imaginary place. You may want to create a place of your own, or draw a map about a place in a book that you like. Don't forget to include a title, **key**, **scale**, and **compass rose**.

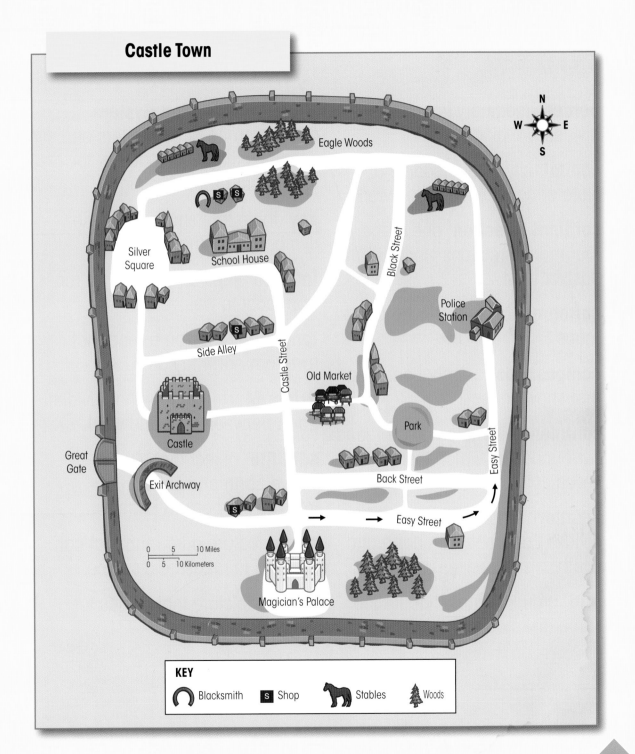

Castle Town

Eagle Woods

Black Street

Silver Square

School House

Police Station

Side Alley

Castle Street

Old Market

Park

Great Gate

Castle

Easy Street

Exit Archway

Back Street

Easy Street

Magician's Palace

N
W E
S

0   5   10 Miles
0   5   10 Kilometers

KEY

Blacksmith   S Shop   Stables   Woods

Glossary

border imaginary line that divides two places

capital city where leaders of a state or country meet and work

cardinal direction one of the four main directions: north, south, east, or west

cartographer person who makes maps

compass rose symbol on a map that shows direction

continent very large area of land surrounded by water; there are seven continents in the world.

Equator imaginary line that divides Earth between north and south

grid group of lines that are the same distance apart

Global Positioning System (GPS) group of computers and satellites that work together to show your exact location

key table that shows what the symbols on a map mean

latitude lines on a map that run from east to west

longitude lines on a map that run from north to south

Prime Meridian line that divides Earth between east and west

satellite object that travels above Earth and sends information back to Earth

scale feature on a map that can be used to measure distance

symbol picture that stands for something else

Find Out More

Organizations and Websites

The Websites below may have some advertisements on them. Make sure to ask a trusted adult to look at them with you. You should never give out personal information online, including your name and address, without first talking to a trusted adult.

American Automobile Association (AAA)
AAA is a group of related automobile clubs. AAA clubs provide free map and direction services to members. Visit **www.aaa.com** to find a AAA club near you, or put AAA and your state name into a trusted search engine.

National Geographic
National Geographic provides free maps and photos of the Earth, as well as interesting articles about people and animals. Visit **www. nationalgeographic.com**.

Yahoo Maps
Find directions from your house to places nearby and far away. Try putting in your address and the address of your school. Do the directions given match your route? **www.maps.yahoo.com**

Books to Read

Baber, Maxwell. *Map Basics*. Chicago: Heinemann Library, 2007.

Junior Classroom Atlas. Chicago: Rand McNally, 2001.

Mahaney, Ian F. *Political Maps*. New York: Rosen, 2007.

Index